BUSES BUILT
BEFORE 1950

ROYSTON MORRIS

AMBERLEY

First published 2021

Amberley Publishing
The Hill, Stroud
Gloucestershire, GL5 4EP

www.amberley-books.com

Copyright © Royston Morris, 2021

The right of Royston Morris to be identified
as the Author of this work has been asserted in
accordance with the Copyrights, Designs and
Patents Act 1988.

ISBN 978 1 3981 0502 7 (print)
ISBN 978 1 3981 0503 4 (ebook)

British Library Cataloguing in Publication Data.
A catalogue record for this book is available from
the British Library.

Origination by Amberley Publishing.
Printed in the UK.

Contents

Introduction

The earliest form of bus transport came in the shape of the horse-drawn omnibus introduced during the nineteenth century, which was basically an upgrade from the stagecoach used in the seventeenth and eighteenth centuries, the main difference being it had a much larger body.

Whereas stagecoaches concentrated on getting people from one destination to another over long distances (with occasional comfort stops on the route – very similar to the nationwide National Express coach services offered to travellers today), the horse-drawn omnibuses would concentrate on an area within a town or city with more frequent stops.

During the 1870s and 1880s, many horse-drawn omnibuses were replaced by steam-operated ones, which were themselves replaced in later years by petrol/diesel vehicles.

Several towns and cities had tramway systems (many originated from horse-drawn through to electric systems), and a large majority of those trams were replaced by electric trolleybuses. These would often utilise the routes already in situ and just changed the overhead wires (from single to double) that were used to run the vehicles along.

During the 1920s through to the 1960s (and into the 1970s) bus travel became a very popular way of getting about, with new operators starting up on a frequent basis. These operators were also regarded as competition to the railway companies around at that time, and saw many rivalries between the two forms of transport – depicted in the 1953 Ealing Studios comedy film *The Titfield Thunderbolt*.

This period also saw the introduction of the charabanc trip. This was usually a day out (more often than not to the seaside) for the villagers or employees of the larger private estates in the country, which led to special vehicles being constructed for that purpose.

When the Dr Beeching cuts was implemented by the government on Britain's railways in the mid-1960s, many outlying towns/small villages and communities lost a major – and at times the only – means of public transport. Many bus operators were also going out of business due to a downturn in customers and not being able to compete with the railways during the late 1940s and early 1950s. Bus companies of today offering regular (even though it may be hourly or less frequent) services to those areas means bus travel is fairly reasonably well supported now, although not as much as it was during the period between the two world wars and the immediate decade following the Second World War.

1
Horse-drawn Omnibuses

In 1824 John Greenwood was the keeper of a toll gate at Pendleton on the Manchester to Liverpool turnpike. He decided to buy a horse and cart, which he fitted with several seats, and started carrying passengers between the two north-western cities. It is because of this that he has been cited as the pioneer for horse-drawn omnibus services in the UK.

There were two main types of these vehicles, which were the 'knifeboard' and 'garden seat' types. The former is so called because the upper-deck seating was arranged so that passengers would be looking to the sides, therefore resembling the shape of a Victorian kitchen utensil used for sharpening knives. The latter had forward-facing seats placed in rows behind each other, and was the more popular of the two types.

Travelling by omnibus differed from stagecoach travel in that no prior booking was required and the driver could pick up/set down anywhere on request, and they were more localised than the longer stagecoach journeys.

As the nineteenth century rolled on, so travelling by omnibus became increasingly popular. It led to much competition between the various operators, which sometimes led to acts of violence or even sabotage, and murder in some exceptional cases. It is hardly surprising that surviving vehicles are very few in number.

On 20 October 2019, at the London Bus Museum, this picture was taken of a *c.* 1875 London General Omnibus Company 4-light knifeboard bus – the '4-light' refers to the number of windows along each side. It perfectly shows off the position of the knifeboard seating on the upper deck. Worth noting is the rope attached to a wide leather belt that would wrap around the driver's waist, preventing him from falling or being pushed off.

This 1886 London Omnibus Co. Ltd twenty-six-seat 'garden seat' bus is on display during a public open day on 27 April 2019 at the Acton Town store of the Transport for London Museum.

This 1890 garden seat version built by Barker & Son is on display at the Stockwood Discovery Centre in Luton – home to the largest private collection of horse-drawn vehicles. Note the Lipton's Tea and Watney's Ale advertising boards in this 10 June 2017 picture.

Solomon Andrews & Son (Francis) were renowned builders and operators of horse-drawn omnibuses. They ran the Andrews Omnibus Company, which was taken over in 1899 by the Star Omnibus Company, who operated fifteen routes in London with a fixed fare of 1*d*. This example of a 3-light garden seat type was built by Solomon in 1890 and was pictured at the London Bus Museum on 20 October 2019.

Another vehicle built by Solomon Andrews & Son in 1890 (this one in Cardiff) was this 4-light garden seat. During the 1940s Dolland & Aictchison, the opticians, used it for promotional publicity purposes. Worth noting is the advertisement on the top side. George Borwick was a Lancashire man who began selling baking powder in 1844; it was the highest-selling baking powder in the world for many years. Pictured on 20 October 2019 at the London Bus Museum.

Built in 1890 by the Manchester Carriage & Tramways Company as No. L2 is this unique 7-light garden seat version. It is the only surviving horse bus from that company and can be seen on display at the Greater Manchester Museum of Transport, where it was pictured on 26 January 2013. Note the spiral staircase at the rear. It was withdrawn from service in 1914 and the horses were requisitioned for army service.

One of the most popular items featured at the 2019 London Bus Museum Transportfest event, held on 20 October, was this beautifully restored and working 1906-built 4-light knifeboard example that was giving rides around the complex and surrounding area, pulled by two magnificently turned out and well-behaved white mares.

In 1828, thirty-one-year-old coachbuilder George Shillibeer visited Paris and was so impressed with their horse-drawn bus service that upon his return to London he built an omnibus that could seat twenty-two people. On 4 July 1829, he began running his own omnibus service between Paddington and Bank, which was the start of buses operating in the capital. In 1929, to celebrate the 100th anniversary of London's buses, apprentices of the LGOC built this replica of George's original vehicle. It was seen in the Transport for London Covent Garden Museum on 15 December 2012.

This ten-seater bus was operated by Lawson's in Glasgow as a station bus, ferrying passengers between the city's two railway stations during the early years of the twentieth century. It is pictured at the Glasgow Riverside Transport Museum on 28 March 2016.

Built in the 1880s for the London & North Western Railway as a 3-light knifeboard type, following its withdrawal in the early 1900s its body was sold and used as a summer house in a Coventry garden until its discovery and removal during the 1980s. It is seen here on display at the Midland Railway Centre in Derbyshire on 16 September 2017.

2
Steam Buses

Following on from the invention of the steam-powered railway locomotive during the mid-1820s, and by the time the 1830s had come around Walter Hancock and associates of the renowned surgeon, chemist and scientist Sir Goldsworthy Gurney had begun running steam-powered buses on the roads of the UK. These vehicles were praised because they were faster than horse buses, far more reliable, less likely to overturn and didn't damaged the roads to the extent that horse-drawn vehicles did.

The major downsides regarding steam bus travel were heavy tolls imposed by the Turnpike Acts. The 1861 Locomotive Act restricted powered vehicles to 5 mph in towns and cities and 10 mph in the countryside (most steam-powered buses could reach speeds of 24 mph). In 1865 the infamous 'Red Flag Act' was introduced on Britain's roads, which reduced speeds down to 2 mph in towns and cities and 4 mph in the countryside, as well as requiring a man bearing a red flag to precede every vehicle on the road. This act was finally repealed in 1896, when steam bus manufacturing increased on a huge scale. Sadly though, out of all of the road steam vehicles that are preserved, the number of steam buses is extremely poorly represented in that area; while some new-build replicas are beginning to appear, they will not replace the originals.

Built in 1902 by Thornycroft Ltd at Basingstoke is this thirty-six-seater coke-powered double-decker steam bus. It was operated by the London Road Car Co. Ltd, but this was only for a short period of time between March and May 1902. It was used in the 2010 film *The Wolfman*, starring Anthony Hopkins, before being converted into a static ice-cream parlour on Liverpool's Albert Dock where it was photographed during a quiet period on 17 July 2016.

Edwin Foden, Sons & Co. of Sandbach in Cheshire are renowned for the manufacturing of commercial vehicles; however, during the late nineteenth and early twentieth centuries they also produced numerous steam lorries and buses. Pictured here at dusk on 4 September 2010 at the Great Dorset Steam Fair in Tarrant Hinton is *Irene*, a 1914-built steam lorry (works No. 4258), which was converted by Foden to carry members of their workforce to and from the factory to the nearby railway station.

Another Foden-built steam bus noted at the Great Dorset Steam Fair on 4 September 2010, giving passengers rides around the site, was works No. 11340, built in 1923 and carrying the name *Puffing Billy*. It was owned by the Rock Ales Company in Brighton and conveyed members of the public and VIPs around the town until the brewery closed in 1928.

Elizabeth (works No. 8590) has had an interesting life. She started at the Sentinel Waggon Works factory in Shrewsbury in 1931 as a type DG6P steam flatbed lorry, before being converted into a tar sprayer. In 1962 she was spotted languishing in a scrapyard when she was acquired for preservation and reverted back to original flatbed. The tourism operator Northern Star Motor Carriage Company converted the lorry into a thirty-seater passenger-carrying steam bus. It operated in this capacity in and around Whitby for thirteen years before being acquired by Crosville Motors in Weston-Super Mare, where it was pictured on 28 August 2015.

Another steam bus built by Sentinel in 1932 is works No. 8714. Noted here on 30 August 2014 at the Great Dorset Steam Fair at Tarrant Hinton, where it was ready to start the day giving rides to visitors around the site during the bank holiday weekend.

Sentinel works No. 9151 relates to this S4 type 1934-built steam bus, pictured here on 15 July 2005 at the annual Somerset Steam Spectacular show, which takes place near the town of Langport.

3

Trolleybuses

On 29 April 1882, Dr Ernst Werner Siemens demonstrated his 'Elektromote' in a suburb of Berlin. This was essentially a converted four-wheel landau horse-drawn carriage that was fitted with two 2.2-kw electric motors that directed power to the rear wheels of the vehicle by means of a chain drive. The erecting of the masts and overhead 550-v DC cable began in 1881. The power to the vehicle was by means of a pole centrally placed within the landau. This was connected to a flexible cable pulling a small eight-wheeled 'Kontaktwagen' that ran along the overhead cables. This wagon, or contact car, was weighted to prevent it from falling off the cables. Power to the cables was by means of a nearby shed that was converted to a power station, using a steam engine hooked up to a dynamo. The Elektromote could travel at 7 mph, and the three-month period between April and June were only regarded as demonstration runs. It signaled the beginning of the trolleybus era.

In the UK the cities of Leeds and Bradford were the first to install trolleybus systems, which began operating in June 1911 and several major towns and cities soon followed them. Ironically, the Bradford system was the last one to operate in Britain, with its closure coming in 1972. Several cities were replacing their tramway systems with trolleybus ones, often utilising the same routes. The major differences were that whereas the tramways would use the track and rails as their return routes, thereby only needing one overhead wire and a single conductor pole, trolleybuses required two overhead wires and two conductor poles fitted to the top of the vehicle to complete the electric circuit. Incidentally, the term Kontaktwagen translated into English as 'trolley', therefore leading to 'trolleybus' (or 'trolley coach', as they became known in some parts of the world).

20 June 1911 saw the first trolleybuses operate in the UK; this took place in Bradford and Leeds. Bradford Tramways Corporation No. 562 is the oldest surviving trolleybus from the Corporation. It was built by the English Electric Company (with their bodywork) in 1929 and was seen undergoing restoration at the Trolleybus Museum in Sandtoft, South Yorkshire on 14 October 2017.

Although there are no public trolleybus systems operating any longer in the UK, there are around 300-plus still operating all over the world. There are a couple of major tourist attractions in the UK that operate small fleets of trolleybuses on a regular basis; these include the East Anglia Transport Museum at Carlton Colville in Suffolk and the National Trolleybus Museum at Sandtoft in South Yorkshire, as well as numerous examples found on display in museums across the country.

14 October 2017 saw 1949-built British United Traction 9611T with East Lancashire Coachbuilders bodywork Bradford No. 834 heading a line of Bradford trolleybuses at the Trolleybus Museum. These are four out of the eleven from Bradford that are preserved at the museum.

There are several trolleybuses from the Bradford Corporation preserved. This 1945 Karrier W type with East Lancashire bodywork (No. 704) was noted at the East Kent Light Railway in Shepherdswell on 19 April 2014 awaiting restoration.

Bradford No. 835 was noted on 19 October 2014 at the North East Land, Sea and Air Museums in Sunderland. Built in 1949 by the British United Traction Company (formed in 1946 as a joint venture between AEC & Leyland), it is a 9611T type fitted with an East Lancashire body. Note the prominence of the two conductor poles on its roof.

Trolleybuses operated in Rotherham, South Yorkshire, for one day short of fifty-three years – 3 October 1912 to 2 October 1965. Noted on 14 October 2017 at the Trolleybus Museum is this 1949-built Daimler CTE6 with a Charles H. Roe Ltd body. It was No. 37 in the Corporation.

This single-decker trolleybus, seen here on 14 October 2017 at the Trolleybus Museum, is in need of some severe restoration work. It was built in 1928 by steam traction engine builders Richard Garrett & Sons at their Leiston works in Suffolk as an O type, and had their own bodywork. It was built for the Mexborough & Swinton Tramways Company as No. 34.

The Wolverhampton system operated between 1923 and 1967. This 1931-built vehicle was constructed by the Wolverhampton firm of Guy Motors Ltd as a BTX type with their bodywork and was given the number '78'. It was seen here, in need of some TLC, at the Black Country Living Museum in Dudley on 29 July 2012. Note the A. J. Stevens three-wheeled delivery van in front of it.

Noted on 26 January 2013 at the Greater Manchester Museum of Transport was one of the 5,500 buses that were built by Crossley Motors Ltd between 1926 and 1958. This example is an Empire TDD42/2, built in 1949 with their bodywork and worked on the Ashton-under-Lyme system as No. 80.

Nottingham Corporation Tramways formed in 1898 and trolleybuses began operating in April 1927; at its peak in 1952 there were 157, before its demise in June 1966. Built in 1949 by British United Traction as a 9611T with Brush Electrical Engineering bodywork was Nottingham No. 506. It was noted at the Trolleybus Museum at Sandtoft on 14 October 2017.

In 2001 a discovery made in Chelmsford, Essex, turned out to be a single-decker trolleybus from Hastings that had been converted into a bungalow – not just the body, but the entire vehicle. It had been purchased in 1949, some ten years before the system closed. Research has revealed that it is a 1929 Guy BTX with Ransomes, Sims & Jefferies bodywork and No. 45. Prior to being purchased it was used as a ticket office at Hastings coach station. On 14 October 2017 it was at the Trolleybus Museum awaiting restoration. Note the tiled apex roof from its days as a bungalow still in situ.

The year 1928 saw the launch of the Maidstone, Kent, trolleybus system, which was to last until 1967. Existing buses from this system are relatively rare. This example noted at the East Anglian Transport Museum on 22 September 2019 was No. 52, which was built in 1949 by British United Traction as a type 9611T with Weymann Ltd bodywork.

Pictured at the Trolleybus Museum on 14 October 2017 is this 1945-built Karrier W type with Charles H. Roe bodywork. It was Doncaster No. 375, whose system operated between 1928 and 1963.

The trolleybus system in London operated for just eight days short of thirty-one years (between May 1931 and May 1962). HX 2756 was built in 1931 by the Associated Equipment Company of Southall as a type 663T with Union Construction Company bodywork, and was London United No. 1. It was pictured at the Transport for London Museum Acton Town storage site on 27 April 2019.

London Transport fleet No. 1201 was built by Leyland Vehicles in 1939 as a LPTB70 with their own bodywork. The LPTB70 was a special type built specifically for London Transport. It was noted in service on 12 August 2007 at the East Anglia Transport Museum at Carlton Colville in Suffolk.

This 1948-built BUT Ltd type 9641T with Metropolitan-Cammell bodywork can usually be seen at the London Bus Museum, but does visit other locations on occasions. On 14 October 2017 it was noted at the Trolleybus Museum in Sandtoft bearing its London Transport number of 1812.

Trolleybuses began operating between Nottingham and Ripley in 1932 (replacing trams that operated on the same route). The system operated until 1953. Only three have survived into preservation. This example – No. 353 – is one of the later ones, built in 1949 by BUT Ltd with Weymann bodywork and seen here at the Trolleybus Museum on 14 October 2017.

Derby Corporation began operating trolleybuses in 1932 and operated 165 vehicles (with a maximum of seventy-three running at any one time). This preserved example was built by Sunbeam as a type W with Park Royal bodywork in 1945. On 14 October 2017 it was at Sandtoft, keeping company with others.

Church Street in Christchurch, Dorset, is the home of a Grade II listed building that formed the trolleybus turntable – just one of five such buildings worldwide. It was used by the Bournemouth Corporation for their Bournemouth to Christchurch system between 1933 and 1969. Built in 1935 as a Sunbeam MS2 with Park Royal bodywork as No. 99, this example was seen on display at the Trolleybus Museum on 14 October 2017.

Another 1935 Sunbeam MS2 with Park Royal bodywork built for the Bournemouth Corporation is this unusual open-topped version (No. 202). It was noted at the East Anglia Transport Museum on 22 September 2019.

Pictured at the Trolleybus Museum following a downpour on 14 October 2017 is Huddersfield Corporation No. 541. It is a 1947 Karrier MS2 with Park Royal body.

On 2 October 1935 Newcastle Corporation introduced trolleybuses to the north-east city. The system closed exactly thirty-one years after it opened, on 2 October 1966. Preserved examples are limited to two or three. This example – No. 501 – was noted at Beamish, the Living Museum of the North, on 19 October 2014. It is a Sunbeam S7 type with Northern Coachbuilders bodywork and dates from 1948.

Between December 1950 and March 1952, the Reading Corporation trolleybus system constantly used sixty-three vehicles. The system itself had been running since 1936 and finally closed in 1963. Five survivors from the Corporation can be found at the Trolleybus Museum in Sandtoft. No. 113 was built in 1939 by AEC as a 661T with Park Royal bodywork. It was noted at the museum on 14 October 2017.

The Railless Electric Traction Co. Ltd was formed in 1908 solely to promote trolleybuses. They had no manufacturing facilities and used chassis supplied by Alldays & Onions Ltd. The South Shields Corporation ran trolleybuses in the north-eastern town between 1936 and 1964. The only surviving vehicle from this system is this example built in 1937 (with Weymann body), as No. 204. It was seen under the wires keeping company with a Bradford vehicle at Sandtoft on 14 October 2017.

Between 1937 and 1960 visitors and residents of the Lincolnshire coastal resort town of Cleethorpes could travel on a trolleybus. Noted devoid of any markings at Sandtoft on 14 October 2017 was No. 54, which has a Park Royal body mounted onto a 1937 AEC 661T chassis.

The Welsh capital city of Cardiff ran trolleybuses that lasted for nearly twenty-eight years (closing in 1970). This example, No. 203, stands at the Trolleybus Museum at the end of a busy day's work on 14 October 2017. It was built when the system opened in 1942 by AEC as a 664T with Northern Counties bodywork.

Looking at this 22 September 2019 picture at the East Anglian Transport Museum, Carlton Colville, it's fairly hard to believe that this trolleybus was built ninety-three years before, in September 1926. It was built by steam manufacturers Richard Garrett & Sons in Lincolnshire as an O type for the NESA-owned (a public utilities electricity distribution company) system in Copenhagen, Denmark. It has Strachan & Brown bodywork and is No. 5.

This vehicle was built in 1932 for the Liège system in Belgium by the Fabrique Nationale d'Armes de Guerre (National Manufacturer of War Weapons), or FN as they were known, with their own bodywork. No. 425 is seen here on 14 October 2017 at the Trolleybus Museum, Sandtoft.

The *réseau de trolleybus de Limoges* has been operating trolleybuses in the French city and surrounding region from 1943 until the present day. The Trolleybus Museum has this preserved example (No. 5, noted on 14 October 2017), which was built in the year that operations began, by the Société des Véhicules et Tracteurs Electriques (a French manufacturer of trolleybuses and electric locomotives). It has Compagnie des Tramways Electriques de Limoges bodywork.

For almost fifty years the South African city of Johannesburg was served by trolleybuses – from August 1936 to January 1986. Pictured at the Trolleybus Museum undergoing a major complete restoration on 14 October 2017 was this 1948 BUT type 9641T with Bus Bodies Ltd bodywork – No. 589.

4
Single-decker Motor Buses

With the introduction of the motorised car towards the end of the nineteenth century and its subsequent popularity moving into the new century, it was inevitable that lorries and buses would be introduced on Britain's roads; however, I don't think that anybody envisaged the impact and change they would have on commerce.

Technically speaking, buses are regarded as commercial vehicles as they can carry more than nine people. And, in a bizarre way, they are. The early motor buses mainly comprised of a lorry chassis with a purpose-built coach body fixed onto it – a practice that, incidentally, is still carried out to this day. There were numerous coachbuilders who made the transition from making bodies that were used on horse-drawn vehicles to those used on trolleybuses, buses and coaches. Several of them became very successful at it, while others would go on to build bodies for Rolls-Royce and Bentley cars, among others.

Many of the early single-deck buses had front ends that looked just like those found on lorries, but sometime during the early 1920s half-cab vehicles started to appear. These allowed the driver to be segregated from the passengers and therefore eliminating him from being distracted. These vehicles survive in vast numbers in the hands of preservationists, museums, etc.

Between 1912 and 1979 the Associated Equipment Company was one of the leading manufacturers of bus, truck and motor coaches. This example was built in 1925 as a type 411 with Strachan & Brown bodywork, and first worked in Newcastle as No. 64. It was noted on 29 August 2011 at the Onslow Park Steam Rally, Shrewsbury.

Taking part in the annual Historic Commercial Vehicle Society's London to Brighton Run on 1 May 2016 and pictured on Brighton Road, Purley, Surrey, was this 1929-built Regal half-cab with LGOC (London General Omnibus Company) body. It was given the number 'T31'.

This 1931-built half-cab Regal (fitted with Duple bodywork) was originally No. T219 with the Green Line company. It was pictured at the Transport for London Museum store at Acton Town on 27 April 2019.

GO 5198 is a former London General half-cab (No. LT1076) that was built in May 1931. It is a Renown with LGOC body fitted. It was pictured on 27 April 2019 at the Acton Town store of the Transport for London Museum.

Built in 1935 as a Q-type chassis complete with Birmingham Railway Carriage & Wagon Company bodywork. This former London Transport No. Q83 was pictured at the 2019 Transportfest event held at the London Bus Museum on 20 October.

W. Alexander & Sons Ltd began running bus services in and around the Fife area in 1913 and became the largest bus operator in Scotland. One of their vehicles (No. A36) is this 1947-built Regal I, which has their own design body. It can be seen at the Scottish Vintage Bus Museum in Lathalmond and was pictured there on 31 March 2013.

This 1948 Regal III with Park Royal bodywork was operated by the Great Northern Railway of Ireland as No. 427. It was pictured at the private offsite store of the Ireland National Transport Museum on 17 April 2017 awaiting restoration.

Pictured at Norton Fitzwarren on 1 August 2009 at the annual West Somerset Railway Associations' Steam Fayre & Vintage Vehicles Rally is this 1948-built Regal III with Strachan body (formerly Crosville Motor Services No. TA5).

The Vintage Bus Running Day event held in Taunton attracted visitors and buses from many different parts of the country. The second, held on Sunday 11 May 2014, was no exception and pictured at it was this Eccles-based 1947 Regal III with Windover Ltd bodywork. This vehicle was originally used by Trent Buses as No. 611.

Hull Corporation Transport No. 5 is a 1949-built half-cab Regal III with Weymann body. It was seen in the Steetlife Museum of Kingston-upon-Hull on 6 October 2018.

This Regal III with Duple bodywork was built in 1949 and is on display in the Oxford Bus Museum, representing an as found semi-derelict example. It was originally used by the South Midland Bus Company as No. 66 and was pictured on 11 November 2019.

The Albion Motor Car Co. Ltd was founded in 1899 and was renamed in 1931 to Albion Motors Ltd. Bus production started in 1923. LJ 9501 is a 1934-built Valiant SpPV70 with Harrington bodywork and was No. 57 with the Bournemouth company Charlie's Cars. It was noted at the Great Dorset Steam Fair at Tarrant Hinton on 3 September 2010.

This 1935 Albion Victor PK114 with Abbott body was unique in that it wasn't owned by a bus operator; instead, it was owned by the landlord and the patrons of the King Alfred public health in Winchester and used by them on annual outings and special occasions. It was seen at the Scottish Vintage Bus Museum in Lathalmond on 31 March 2013, a long way from its former home.

In 1925 Vauxhall Motors was acquired by General Motors, but they continued trading using the Vauxhall brand. In 1931 they began commercial vehicle building under the marque of 'Bedford'. Built in 1932 is this WLB type with Davies Ltd bodywork, which was built for Williams in Blaina. It was pictured in Purley, Surrey, on 1 May 2016 while taking part in the annual HCVS London to Brighton Run. Note some of the other vehicles taking part behind it.

The Bedford OB is instantly recognisable to most enthusiasts, and this former Clifton College, Bristol (No. 219), example is no exception. It was built in 1949 with Mulliner bodywork and was pictured taking part in the Taunton Vintage Bus Running Day on 10 May 2015.

This 1949-built Bedford OB has been fitted with Duple bodywork with semi-open sides. It was first used by Western National as No. 1413. It is pictured here on 31 October 2015 at the Regent Street Motor Show in London. The following day it was driven in the 60-mile London to Brighton Veteran Road Run by the radio and television celebrity Chris Evans as a prize for those people who had donated the most to the BBC Children in Need appeal auction on his Radio 2 Breakfast Show.

Bristol Commercial Vehicles began building buses in 1908 and lasted until 1981. Western National No. 172 is one of those vehicles. It was built in 1935 as a JJW6A type with Beadle bodywork and was noted at the West of England Transport Collection open day at Winkleigh, Devon, on 6 October 2013.

This 1949 former Bristol Omnibus Company (No. 2447) L5G half-cab with Eastern Coach Works body heads along Brighton Road, Purley, during the annual HCVS London to Brighton Run on 12 May 2019.

The North Western Road Car Co. Ltd was based in Stockport and operated buses between 1923 and 1974. Pictured at Taunton during the Vintage Bus Running Day on 10 May 2015 was former NW fleet No. 206, a 1949-built Bristol type L5G half-cab with Weymann bodywork.

Bristol Omnibus Company No. 2467 is a 1949-built L6B type with ECW body and was pictured on 11 September 2016 within the grounds of the Helicopter Museum at Weston-super-Mare during a classic cars and vintage bus rally event.

Pictured on 6 May 2013, on a bright and sunny day at the Abbey Hill Steam Rally in Yeovil, Somerset, was former Hants & Dorset No. 677, which is a 1949 ECW-bodied Bristol LL6B model. Note the unusual specifically designated place for the fire extinguisher.

Built in 1949 for Albert Davies Ltd of Acton Burnell in Shropshire by Crossley Motors Ltd is this SD42/7 type with Plaxton bodywork fitted. Pictured at the Onslow Park Steam Rally in Shrewsbury on 29 August 2011.

This vehicle, which dates from 1920, is a Daimler Y chassis with a City of Oxford Electric Tramways Company body (formerly No. 39). It was noted in an 'unrestored as found condition' inside the Oxford Bus Museum at Long Hanborough on 11 November 2019.

Apart from cars, Daimler are also well known for building buses. This 1949-built CVD6SD half-cab type with Weymann body first saw service with the Exeter Corporation as No. 73. On 10 May 2015 it was seen taking part in the Taunton Vintage Bus Running Day.

Between 1903 and 1972 Dennis Brothers Ltd of Guildford in Surrey built lorries, buses and fire engines. This example was built in 1929 for the West Bromwich Corporation as No. 32. It is an ES type with Dixon Bros bodywork, and was pictured at the Black Country Living Museum in Dudley on 29 July 2012.

Edwin Foden Sons & Co. Ltd were founded in Sandbach, Cheshire, in 1887, where they manufactured large industrial and small stationary steam engines, traction engines, etc., before moving on to lorries and buses. This example is a 1949 type PVSC6 with bodywork built by Lawton & Company and was originally used by the Coppenhall Brothers in Sandbach. It was pictured at the Greater Manchester Museum of Transport on 26 January 2013.

Guy Motors Ltd, founded in 1914, were specialists in manufacturing commercial vehicles (they also made three models of cars between 1919 and 1924). During the 1914–18 war, under the control of the Ministry of Munitions, every vehicle produced would be used for military use. Civil production began in 1919.

Pictured at a private collection in West Yorkshire on 13 August 2016 is this 1938 Wolf with Waveney Ltd bodywork. New to Llandudno, North Wales, it would take tourists up to the top of the Great Orme. Note the Native American head on top of the radiator, which was the company's chosen logo.

Seen undergoing restoration work on the same date and location as the previous picture is this former Premier Buses of Keighley vehicle. It was built by Karrier in 1925 as a JH type and is fitted with Strachan & Brown Bodywork. Karrier was the trading name used by Clayton & Co. of Huddersfield.

Another vehicle from the same private collection (also on the same date) is this 1928 Karrier WL6 type fitted with an English Electric body. It was first used by the Ashton-under-Lyme Corporation Tramways & Motors Company as No. 8. Note the clerestory-style roof, which is usually found on railway carriages.

In 1896 the Lancashire Steam Motor Company was founded in the town of Leyland. In 1907 the company had been renamed to Leyland Motors Ltd and they would go on to being one of the largest manufacturers of commercial vehicles in the UK. This S4.36.T3 type with their own bodywork was built in 1914 for the LNWR to operate from their base at Crewe as No. 59. On 10 June 2018 it was pictured at a private collection in Bedfordshire.

One of the most successful vehicles built by Leyland was the Lion. This 1927 LSC1 type was new to Ribble Motor Services in Preston and was fitted with their bodywork and given the number '295'. It was pictured at the Greater Manchester Museum of Transport on 26 January 2013.

This Lion is a type LT1 that was built in 1929 for the Sunderland Corporation as No. 2. It has Leyland bodywork and was pictured on 9 July 2011 at the Southern Industrial History Trust Museum at Amberley in West Sussex.

This Lion LT5 type with Weymann body has seen much better days as it awaits patiently for restoration work to commence at the West of England Transport Collection in Winkleigh on 6 October 2013. This vehicle was new to the Devon General Company in 1933 as No. 68.

More successful and popular than the Lion was the Leyland Tiger. This type TS4 half-cab with Santus Ltd bodywork was built in 1932 for the Wigan Corporation (No. 81). It is pictured at Winkleigh on a sunny autumnal 6 October 2013.

The weather was exceptionally good for the Taunton Vintage Bus Running Day held on 8 May 2016. Seen soaking up the sun is this former Exeter Corporation No. 66, a 1938-built Tiger TS8 with bodywork made by Cravens Ltd.

Taken the same day as the previous image (also at Taunton) is this 1949 Tiger type PS2/3 with Burlingham Brothers body, its yellow livery shining resplendently in the bright spring sunshine. It was new to the Bournemouth Corporation in that year as No. 44.

On a rather wet 21 May 2016 I was pleasantly surprised to see this 1949-built Tiger type PS1/1 with bodywork by Weymann parked up on the main road approach to Wellington town centre in Somerset.

Pictured at the London Bus Museum on 20 October 2019 during the annual Transportfest event was this former London Transport (No. C94) 1936-built Leyland Cub KP03 type with Weymann body.

Brighton Road in Purley, Surrey, on a bright 12 May 2019 was the location for this 1937 Cub KPZ2 with Park Royal body, as it takes part in the HCVS London to Brighton Run. It was new to Southdown as No. 24.

This unusual-looking specimen is a Leyland REC with London Passenger Transport Board bodywork. It was built for London Transport in 1939 and numbered 'CR16'. It was seen at Brooklands on 20 October 2019.

The Maudslay Motor Company was founded in 1901, originally to build marine internal-combustion engines; however, by 1902 they had started to make cars, followed by buses a year later. They remained in business in Coventry until 1948. One of their surviving buses is this dust-covered example seen at Winkleigh on 4 October 2015. It was built in 1931 as a ML3BC/4LW with Thurgood Ltd bodywork for Church Brothers in Pytchley, Northamptonshire.

In 1909 the Ford Motor Company (England) came into existence. During the 1914–18 conflict they expanded from cars into making commercial vehicles under the Fordson name. After the Second World War they made these vehicles under the brand name of Thames.

This ET6 type with Scottish Aviation bodywork was built in 1949 for Ganson Brothers of Lerwick and was noted on 29 August 2011 at the Onslow Park Steam Rally in Shrewsbury.

In 1909 Thomas Tilling Ltd merged with W. A. Stevens and produced buses and commercial vehicles under the Tilling-Stevens name until 1950. This 1932 Express B39A7 type with Beadle bodywork was new to Western National (No. 3379). It was seen at Winkleigh on 6 October 2013 awaiting restoration.

5
Double-deck Motor Buses

The idea of a vehicle having two decks can be traced back to the 1840s when passengers could travel inside or, if they were feeling brave, on the outside atop the horse-drawn omnibuses. Access to the upper deck was via a single semi-spiral staircase at the rear of the vehicle. There was no roof covering and no safety belts/straps to prevent the passengers from falling off.

Over the course of time, however, the double-deck vehicles would develop considerably, leading to a fully enclosed upper deck. The first types had the half-cab seen on the later versions of the single-decker buses. In time, both types would have the cab enclosed within the structure of the body, and eventually an extremely large panoramic front window would be included on these vehicles (but those are outside of the period that this book covers). Surviving vehicles are numerous, but apparently around half as many as single-decker buses.

This AEC NS type with LGOC bodywork was seen during an open day at the Acton Town store of the Transport for London Museum on 27 April 2019. It was built for the LGOC in 1927 and numbered 'NS 1995'.

Built in 1931 as No. ST 821 for the LGOC (whose bodywork it carries) is this AEC Regent. It was seen at Acton Town store on 27 April 2019. Note the unusual front overhang on the top deck.

During the Second World War, London was obviously a major target for the German bombers. At the London Bus Museum this former London Transport (No. STL 2093) 1937-built Regent with LPTB bodywork (seen on 20 October 2019) is part of a display giving some idea of the damage caused by the incendiaries that fell on the city.

Parked up at the 20 October 2019 Transportfest event at the London Bus Museum is this Regent III with Cravens Ltd body. It was new to London Transport in 1949 as No. RT 1431. Note the route number indicator box, which is high up on the roofline.

Pictured at a private collection in Essex on 3 April 2010 was this 1949 Regent III with Weymann bodywork. New to London Transport (No. RT 3241), it was undergoing major restoration work and will take a lot more of it before it looks anything like the next image.

This resplendent-looking, beautifully restored 1949 Weymann-bodied Regent III was noted at the East Anglian Transport Museum at Carlton Colville on 22 September 2019. New to London Transport, it formed part of their London Country routes services as No. RT 3125.

Former Glasgow Corporation No. B92 was built at the Biggar, South Lanarkshire, works of Albion Motors in 1937 as a Venturer CX37S type with bodywork by Croft Brothers Ltd. It can currently be seen on display in the Glasgow Riverside Transport Museum, where it was pictured on 28 March 2016.

New to the Bristol Omnibus Company in November 1940 was this Bristol-built type K5G (with their own bodywork). It was given the number of 'C3336' and was seen on display at Winkleigh on 6 October 2013. Note the prominent slope of the front.

Another 1940-built K5G (this one with an ECW body) is former Brighton, Hove & District example, No. 6352. It was noted at the Claude Jessett Trust's Great Bush Narrow Gauge Railway at Hadlow Down in East Sussex on 4 August 2012.

On display during the 8 May 2016 Vintage Bus Running Day in Taunton was this 1945 Bristol-built K6A type with ECW body. It was originally used as No. 353 by Western National. Note the hand winders for changing the destination boards.

Just making it into this book is this former Western National (No. 959) Bristol K6B with bodywork by ECW. It was built in December 1949 and was seen at Winkleigh on 4 October 2015.

This 1949 Bristol KSW6G type is one of many that were fitted with ECW bodywork. It was new to Bristol Omnibus Company as No. 8336 and was noted at Taunton bus station during the Vintage Running Day held on 11 May 2014.

In 1934 Crossley Motors built this Mancunian for the Manchester Corporation, which was fitted with bodywork designed by both parties and numbered '346'. Following its withdrawal from service it was used as a mobile caravan for many years. On 26 January 2013 it was on display at the Greater Manchester Museum of Transport undergoing restoration.

Vintage bus running days held across the country attract large numbers of enthusiasts and often see visiting vehicles that operated from far away. This was the case in Taunton, Somerset, on 11 May 2014 when this 1949 Crossley-built DD42/7 type with Roe bodywork was in attendance. It was new to Woods of Mirfield in West Yorkshire as No. 20.

CCX 777 was built in 1945 by Daimler as a type CW6A with Duple bodywork for the Huddersfield Corporation (No. 217). It was noted in Taunton on 10 May 2015 carrying London Transport livery No. D 130. Note the unusual shape of the bodywork on the upper front corners.

Dundee Corporation No. 127 was built in 1949 as a Daimler CVD6DD type with Croft Brothers body. It was noted at the Dundee Museum of Transport on 28 March 2016.

G 531 was new to London Transport in February 1946. It is a GUY Arab II with Park Royal body and was seen on 20 October 2019 during the Transportfest event at the London Bus Museum.

Burton-on-Trent Corporation No. 16 is a 1949 GUY Arab III with Massey Ltd bodywork, and was observed at the Bass Museum of Brewing in Burton on 3 August 2007.

The most popular double-deck vehicle built by Leyland Motors Ltd was the Titan. This example, a type TD1 with SBG Engineering bodywork, was new to the Glasgow Corporation in 1928 as No. 111. On 31 March 2013 it was pictured at the Scottish Vintage Bus Museum in Lathalmond.

Southdown Motor Services Ltd operated in East and West Sussex and parts of Hampshire between 1915 and 1969. This 1928 TD1 with Leyland's own body was one of those vehicles (No. 873). It can be found at the Southern Industrial History Trust Museum at Amberley, as was the case on 11 July 2009.

This Leyland-bodied 1938 Titan TD5c was new to the Plymouth Corporation as No. 141. It was seen on display at the Winkleigh open day on 7 October 2012.

This 1940 Titan TD7 with Leyland body was noted on 26 January 2013 at the Greater Manchester Museum of Transport, where it was undergoing restoration work. It was new to Wigan Corporation as No. 70.

Another former Plymouth Corporation Titan was seen at Winkleigh on 4 October 2015. This example is a type PD1 with Roe body, and it was new to the Corporation in June 1946 as No. 89.

Seen soaking up the autumn sunshine at Winkleigh on 4 October 2013 – not in concours condition by a long way though, as it patiently awaits for the restorers to begin their work – is this 1947-built, Leyland-bodied former East Kent Corporation Titan PD1A.

GLJ 957 is a January 1948-built Titan PD1A Lowbridge with ECW body. Its original number was PD 959 when used by Hants & Dorset Motor Services. It was pictured on 4 October 2015 at Winkleigh showing signs that its paintwork was in need of some TLC.

Built by Leyland in the same year as the previous image is this North Western (No. 224) Titan PD2/1 type with Leyland body. It was noted on 26 January 2013 at the Greater Manchester Museum of Transport.

The last vehicle in this chapter was seen on display during the 2019 Transportfest event, on 20 October, held at the London Bus Museum. It is ex-London Transport No. RTL 139, which is a 1949-built Leyland type 7RT with Park Royal bodywork.

6

Charabancs

The charabanc was introduced in France during the 1840s and had up to four or five rows of crosswise bench seats and a slightly lower seat for a groom. Because they could seat reasonable numbers, they were used to attend race meetings and by hunting/shooting parties. The name 'char-a-banc' translates as 'carriage with wooden benches' and they are often mispronounced as 'sharra-bang'. They were long wheel-based vehicles, and in most cases they were open topped (with a folding roof fitted to the more opulent versions). Later, several of them were built with a permanent roof and windows, making them enclosed from the elements.

Their popularity increased significantly during the early years of the twentieth century and lasted through to the 1950s/60s. They were more commonly used to take large parties (often works employees or staff of the local lord) away on a day's outing. Often they were run by pub landlords to take regular customers/local villagers on an annual trip (usually to some seaside resort) and the customers/villagers could pay a couple of pennies a month or so to pay for their fare, if there was any charge that is – sometimes the local gentry would arrange for two or three charabancs to take his workers/local villagers away for the day at no cost to them. They would occasionally have another vehicle following with provisions for the day trippers (usually soft drinks and sandwiches). There are a few survivors left and these are often seen at rallies and open days, with a couple of them still being used by companies offering 'nostalgic charabanc outings' as part of their business.

The George Mossman Collection housed at the Stockwood Discovery Centre in Luton, Bedfordshire, is home to many horse-drawn vehicles. This nine-seater charabanc is one of them, built in 1890 by W. J. Courtman of Garleston in Suffolk. It was licensed to carry passengers in Great Yarmouth, Norfolk, and was noted on 10 June 2017.

In the west of Scotland, on the western shore of Loch Gilp, the little hamlet village of Ardrishaig can be found. It was from here that this nine-seater, horse-drawn charabanc operated, transporting visitors to and from the nearby Kilmory Castle. It was built in 1892 and is on display inside the Glasgow Riverside Museum of Transport, where it was pictured on 28 March 2016.

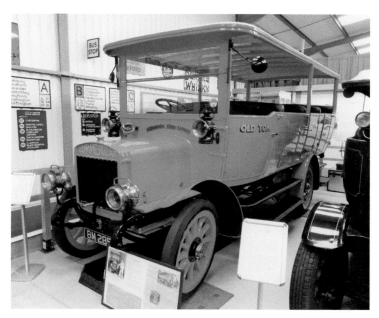

Commercial Cars Ltd was founded in Luton in 1905 and they built buses, charabancs, fire engines , lorries, etc., using the brand name of Commer. This 1914-built example is a WP3 type with their bodywork. It was used by the Earl of Lonsdale to take the workers of his Lowther Hall estate in Westmorland, Cumbria, on yearly outings to Grange-over-Sands during the summer months. It was pictured at the Oxford Bus Museum on 10 November 2019.

In 1897 twin brothers Francis Edgar and Freelan Oscar Stanley, after having sold their photographic dry plate business to the Eastman Kodak Company, built their first steam-powered car. In 1900 they were both general managers with the Locomobile Company of America; however, in 1902 they left and sold the design rights of their cars to the company. They formed the Stanley Motor Carriage Company and rivalled – then went on to overtake – their former employers in steam car production, lasting until 1926.

In 1913 a customer ordered a long wheelbase 30-hp car, but he wanted a charabanc body on it to take friends on shooting parties. The result was this 1914-built, eight-seater pramhood roofed convertible vehicle, noted at the Great Dorset Steam Fair on 5 September 2010.

This Thornycroft vehicle – pictured at the World of Country Life Museum at Sandy Bay, Devon, on 26 August 2007 – was built at the company's Basingstoke factory in July 1919 as a type J2 lorry with a tipper body. In February 1990 it was auctioned in Taunton as part of the Teddy Tucker Collection. By 1992 the new owners had completely refurbished the vehicle, which is now sporting this Peskett Ltd charabanc body and has featured in the television period drama series *Downton Abbey*.

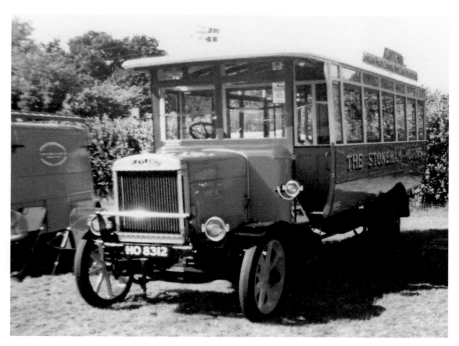

Pictured on a hot and sunny 12 July 2009 at the Sewards Steam and Vintage Gathering in Liss, Hampshire, was this 1921-built Leyland RAF type with Eastbourne Aviation Ltd body, which was new to Stoneham Motors in Eastleigh as No. 5.

New to Edmund Williams Motors in Bromyard, Herefordshire, in 1922 was this Maxwell 25-cwt charabanc. It remained with the Williams family until 1950 when it was sold to Lord Montagu of Beaulieu and now forms part of the National Motor Museum collection, which was where it was noticed on display on 4 August 2019.

The Vulcan Motor & Engineering Co. Ltd was based in Southport, where between 1902 and 1928 they manufactured motor cars, then also commercial vehicles between 1914 and 1953. Former Southdown No. 174 is one of those. It is a type VSD, which was rebodied in 1995 with Peskett bodywork by the owners of the World of Country Life Museum, Sandy Bay, Devon where it was noted on 14 September 2014.

This picture was taken at the South West of England Festival of Transport in Yeovil, Somerset, on 11 August 1991. This vehicle is a 1925-built Morris-Commercial 1-ton that has a replica 1984-built body, due to the original one being in a such a poor condition. It can currently be seen at the Oxford Bus Museum.

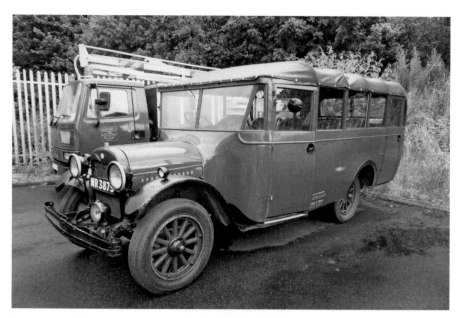

Ransom Eli Olds was born in Ohio in 1864 and in 1905 he founded the REO Motor Car Company in Michigan. The company built mostly cars and lorries; however, in 1925 they built this REO Speed Wagon charabanc for Harrington Motor Services in Fordingbridge, Hampshire. It was seen on 29 July 2012 at the Black Country Living Museum in Dudley, West Midlands.

This immaculately restored Lioness LTB1 with Burlingham bodywork was built by Leyland Motors in 1929 for Brookes Brothers of Rhyl in North Wales as No. 7. It was noted ferrying passengers to and from the nearby (4 miles away) Eggesford railway station for the West of England Transport Collection public open day on 7 October 2012.

New to Fox Motor Services in Alfreton, Derbyshire, in March 1932 was this Commer Centaur with bodywork by Reeves & Kenning Ltd. It was pictured looking in a splendid condition on 13 August 2016 at a private collection in West Yorkshire.

7
Open-topped Motor Buses

These days open-topped double-decker buses are associated with tourist tours or when a team wins a major trophy or competition and they are used to take the team around their home town/city. However, these vehicles have been in existence for well over 100 years. Up until the mid- to late 1920s most of the early double-decker buses that were built had no roof on them, but they did have seats, therefore making them open-topped buses.

Not all open-topped buses are specially built ones; some are converted from regular double-deck buses that might have sustained damaged when striking a low bridge, for example. More often than not these buses have the upper deck removed (or perhaps part of it, usually leaving the front portion of the roof intact) and all are fitted with a guide rail, which is normally around the height of halfway up the sides on the original windows. These are reasonably well represented in terms of preservation.

Viewed from an upper gallery of the Imperial War Museum at Duxford on 2 February 2020 is this AEC type B with LGOC body. It was new to London General as No. B43 in 1911.

LF 8375 is another pre-First World War AEC type B. It was built in 1912 with LGOC bodywork and given the number of 'B1609'. On 1 May 2016 it was pictured on Brighton Road in Purley, Surrey, taking part in the HCVS annual London to Brighton Run. Note the destination board, which predates the hand-wound revolving type.

During 1906 the company of former smith and millwright John Hall, John Hall Engineering Ltd (founded in 1785), began manufacturing commercial vehicles in Dartford using the brand name of Halliford – a combination their founder's surname and the second part of the town's name. They produced these vehicles until 1926.

Seen at the Festival of Steam held at the Historic Royal Chatham Dockyard over the 2014 Easter weekend (Sunday 20 April), was this 3-ton type with Tilling body, which was built for the Maidstone & District Corporation in November 1912.

Built by Tilling-Stevens Ltd as a type TS3 in 1914 for Worthing Motor Services is this Newman Ltd-bodied open topper. It was noted on 9 July 2011 at the Southern Industrial History Trust's Amberley Museum.

Noted on 12 August 2007 at Caister Castle in Great Yarmouth was this 1915 vehicle. It was built by the Locomobile Company of America as a 45-hp lorry for the American army during the First World War. Following its acquisition for preservation it was rebuilt in 1963 using a LGOC body taken from a 1911 vehicle. When seen it was in great need of some TLC.

Some twelve years after the previous image and the bus has now been restored in pristine condition LGOC livery and takes pride of place inside the onsite, purpose-built Motor Museum at Caister Castle, as this picture from 22 September 2019 shows.

Built at Basingstoke in 1919 for the Portsmouth Corporation (as No. 10) is this Thornycroft J type with Dodson Brothers bodywork. It is seen here ninety-five years later back in the town where it was built, at the Milestones Living Museum on 1 March 2014.

LGOC No. K424 was built by AEC in 1920 as a K type with bodywork by Brush of Loughborough, It was noted on 31 October 2015 at the Regent Street Motor Show in London.

Seen on 9 July 2011 ferrying visitors around the Amberley Museum complex is this 1920 Leyland N type with Short Brothers body. It was new to Southdown as No. 125.

This Leyland G2 type with Phoenix Engineering body was built in 1921 for the Todmorden Corporation in West Yorkshire (No. 14). It was noted at a private collection in Bedfordshire on 10 June 2018. Note the registration plate, which bizarrely ascribes the vehicle as being a 'Hackney Carriage'.

The AEC type S was the main stalwart vehicle of the London General Omnibus Company for many years. This 1922 example with Dodson Ltd bodywork was No. S454 when new, and it was pictured at the London Bus Museum on 20 October 2019.

Short Brothers of Belfast were known for their aircraft building and 'flying-boat' designs. They also made bodywork for buses, albeit on a much smaller scale than the aircraft production. This 1922 Leyland N type Special has one of their bodies on it, and it was new to Southdown as No. 135. It was noted at the premises of the Scottish Vintage Bus Museum in Lathalmond on 31 March 2013.

Another former LGOC AEC type S (No. S742) is this 1923-built example with Ransomes of Ipswich body. It was noted on display at the British Motor Museum at Gaydon on 16 December 2018.

London Bus Route 11 is one of the oldest to have run continuously in the city – over 100 years. It was introduced by the LGOC in August 1906 and still runs these days. In 1922 the general manager of the LGOC got together with coachbuilder Christopher Dodson Ltd and they introduced the Leyland LB (London Bus) type vehicles on the route. The livery of these vehicles was brown and cream and they were branded 'Express', earning them the unflattering nickname of 'Chocolate Express'. This 1924 LB5 type (No. B6) was pictured at the Acton Town store of the Transport for London Museum on 27 April 2019.

The offsite storage location of the National Transport Museum of Ireland has numerous vehicles all in various states of disrepair and awaiting restoration, including this 1949 AEC Regent III with Park Royal bodywork, which was seen there on 17 April 2017. It was new to the Morecambe and Heysham Corporation as No. 58, and was transferred to Ireland during the mid-1960s.

Not something you see every day: an open-topped bus loaded with passengers and being driven around a racetrack. This was the scene on 25 June 2016 at the Castle Combe Circuit in Wiltshire during an action day held there. This Bristol K5G type with ECW body was new to the Bristol Corporation as No. C3315 in March 1941.

8

Service and Specialist Vehicles

A large majority of bus companies and operators had various service vehicles, which were an essential part of keeping their fleet of buses operating. They came in very diverse forms and some of these are featured in this chapter. The most common types of these vehicles found today are the first two categories covered here.

Tower Wagons

Tower wagons were vehicles that would grant engineers and maintenance workers access to the overhead cables used by trolleybuses (and trams), with many being retained from the tramcar era for that very reason. They were mainly comprised of a hydraulic scissor lift with a flat platform on the top, all of which was fitted to either the rebuilt chassis of an existing bus or they were purpose built by companies that specialised in their manufacture.

The oldest vehicle that can be seen at the Trolleybus Museum at Sandtoft is this former Reading Corporation Tramways horse-drawn tower wagon. It was built in 1902, a year after the tramway began operations. It was seen here at the museum, on display in the autumn sunshine, on 14 October 2017.

On display on 6 August 2007 at the Tramway Village and National Tram Museum in Crich, Derbyshire, was this 1911-built horse-drawn tower wagon. It was built for the City of Manchester Tramways Company.

Pictured on 23 June 2012 during an open day held at the Abbey Pumping Station in Leicester was this 1911-built Leyland tower wagon, made for the Leicester Corporation Tramways.

Founded 1809 in Ipswich, Suffolk, as Ransome & Son (later to become Ransomes, Sims & Jefferies Ltd) as manufacturers of general engineering products ranging from lawnmowers to steam engines. Pictured at the East Anglian Transport Museum in Carlton Colville on 22 September 2019 was this unusual battery-electric tower wagon that was built by the company in 1922.

New to Bournemouth Corporation in 1934 as No. 12 was this AEC-built Regent tower wagon, seen at Winkleigh during a West of England Transport Collection open day held on 6 October 2013.

London Transport No. 890 was allocated to the Manor House depot of the Electrical Equipment Engineer. It is a 1936 AEC Mercury purpose-built overhead wire repair tower wagon, and was seen at the Transport for London Acton Town store on 27 April 2019.

Pictured at the Helicopter Museum in Weston-Super-Mare on 11 September 2016 was former Bristol Onmibus Corporation tower wagon No. W75. It was new to the Corporation in 1938 and has been built on a Bristol L5G chassis.

During the last public running day on 14 October 2017 at the Trolleybus Museum, doing repair work to an overhead cable carrying post, is this AEC Regent tower wagon. It was built in 1939 for the Nottingham Corporation Tramways as No. 802.

On 9 July 2016 at the Wirral Transport & Tramway Museum, Birkenhead, this former Liverpool Corporation Tramways tower wagon was seen. It is a GUY Vixen and was new to the Corporation when built in 1946. It was used for overhead wiring maintenance until 1957, when it was then used exclusively for street lighting work. It is now part of the museum's back-up overhead maintenance fleet.

EKY 954 is a 1947-built Karrier CK3 type tower wagon, built in 1947 for the Bradford Corporation as No. O34. It was pictured at the Trolleybus Museum on 14 October 2017 where it was awaiting some TLC and light restoration work to be done.

Seen at the Greater Manchester Museum of Transport on 26 January 2013 was this former Bolton Corporation Transport (No. 367) 1948-built Leyland Titan PD2/4 double-decker, which had been converted to a tower wagon.

On 11 February 2012 this immaculate-looking 1949-built Bedford OLAZ vehicle with tower wagon body by Eagle Ltd was on display at the South Yorkshire Transport Museum at Aldwarke. After the Rotherham trolleybuses stopped running in 1965 this vehicle was used mainly to gain access to the clock tower in the town centre, and also as an apprentice training vehicle before being preserved in 1984.

The West of England Transport Collection at Winkleigh on 4 October 2015 saw a rather dilapidated-looking former Plymouth City Transport 1949-built Bedford KZ tower wagon in much need of a restoration job.

Recovery Vehicles and Mobile Cranes

Most of the recovery vehicles that were found in bus garages and depots were converted from buses for the purpose they were to be used for. The heavy-duty recovery vehicles were no exception in this. They had to be large and strong enough to go to the rescue of the biggest buses on the road (mainly double-deckers), so converting the same type of vehicles for this purpose made perfect sense and it saved the company money by having to either hire or purchase a heavy-duty breakdown recovery lorry. Several of these vehicles were formerly used by the military as gun or tank tractors, and so also made for a good investment by the company/operator.

This was built in 1938 for the Hants & Dorset Motor Services as No. 9081 and as a Bristol L5G double-decker; however, following its conversion to a heavy recovery vehicle it was reclassified as a 6LW. It was pictured at Winkleigh on 6 October 2013.

This recovery vehicle began its working life as a Leyland Titan TD5 for Southdown as No. 0184 in 1938. Seen on 1 May 2016 in Purley, Surrey, where it was being used as an emergency recovery vehicle for vehicles taking part in the annual HCVS London to Brighton Run.

LSU 282 was built by AEC as a Matador 0853 type in 1943 for the British army as a heavy-duty artillery and tank-towing tractor. During the 1950s it was purchased by Lancashire United and converted to a recovery breakdown vehicle. On 26 January 2013 it was seen at the Greater Manchester Museum of Transport.

This example, seen at the Cavan & Leitrim Light Railway at Dromod in the Republic of Ireland on 26 April 2018, is a converted 1949 Leyland Tiger OPS3/1. It was formerly Irish Rail No. P164.

This was built by GUY Motors of Wolverhampton in 1944 as an Arab II double-decker, and was No. 40 with the Bournemouth Corporation. In 1952 it became an open topper for the summertime seafront services. Ten years later it was fitted with a Jones 'Super 20' crane and used for the lifting and planting of the trolleybus traction poles. It was pictured during 2002 (exact date not recorded) during a lifting demonstration at the Yellow Buses depot open day in Bournemouth.

Breakdown Tenders

These vehicles were converted from both single- and double-decker buses where the original body was scrapped and replaced with new purpose-built ones. Although they were equipped for light towing (not double-deckers) they were seldom used for that purpose, with most companies preferring to send them out on a breakdown and see whether the problem could be resolved at the roadside. They were also deployed alongside the recovery vehicle with a mechanic on board, as they contained a plethora of equipment that could be required to resolve the problem with the stricken vehicle they were attending.

You might miss this gem hidden among the undergrowth at the Amberley Museum. It is a 1927 Albion PM28 with Beadle body, which was converted to a breakdown tender and was used as a house upon withdrawal from service. It is preserved depicting the similar condition it was found in. Note the bathroom extractor fan on this 9 July 2011 photograph.

AGX 520 was built by AEC in 1933 as a Regent I with LGOC bodywork, rebuilt in 1944 after suffering bomb damage. In 1949 the body was scrapped and it was fitted with a Chalmers of Redhill, Surrey, breakdown tender body and numbered '738J' by London Transport. It was noted on 20 October 2019 at the Brooklands Museum.

Another London Transport-converted AEC-built Regent I is this 1934 example, which was rebodied with Chalmers bodywork in 1950 to Fleet No. 830J. It was noted on 27 April 2019 at the Transport for London Acton Town store.

Grit Wagons

Again, grit wagons were vehicles that were converted. The bodies were removed and replaced by newly built ones specific to the task that was required. These wagons were fitted with boxes that could contain grit and salt, and had a mechanism that was operated from the driver's cab in order to dispense it underneath the body onto the roads – similar to road gritters used today. These unusual vehicles were also fitted out with a special detergent and sand boxes, which would be used if a bus was involved in a traffic accident that might result in a diesel spillage on the highway. The detergent would be spread across the area affected and the sand would then be applied to soak up and remaining fluid.

A visit the South Yorkshire Transport Museum at Aldwarke should result in seeing two former Sheffield Corporation AEC Regents that have been converted to gritter wagons. The first of these is the 1941 Regent I (No. G54), which was seen there on 11 February 2012.

The second converted gritting wagon at Aldwarke is this 1948-built Regent III (No. G55), seen on the same date as the previous image. Both of these vehicles were converted from double-deck buses and fitted with equipment underneath the chassis that would spray salt/grit onto the icy Sheffield streets.

Tree Lopers

One of the problems experienced by bus operators for many years has been tree branches and overhanging vegetation, which can cause obstructions to the driver and can damage windows, mirrors, etc. These obstacles were rarely cleared away by local authorities or highways agencies. Some operators overcame this by utilising an open-topped vehicle, as this was the easiest to convert. It only involved removing the seats from the upper deck, so it could therefore be reverted to passenger use. Some companies, however, converted double-decked vehicles, which meant removing the top part of the roof and the seats. Aside from the cost of converting these types of vehicles, the other negative aspect was they could not be reconverted back to their original forms, which is why most operators preferred the open-top option for those operations.

The City of Oxford Corporation converted this open-topped double-decker into a tree loper by removing the seats from the upper deck to allow room for the cut-off branches and roadside vegetation. Upon its withdrawal the seats were refitted. This example (No. 16), pictured at the Oxford Bus Museum at Long Hanborough on 10 November 2019, is a 1932 AEC Regent I with Brush Engineering body.

This Leyland Titan TD4 with English Electric Company bodywork was new to the Portsmouth Corporation (No. 8) in 1935. It was converted to a tree loper – note the piece of equipment that was used for this purpose, just sticking out above the open-top deck. This picture was taken at the Milestones Museum in Basingstoke on 1 March 2014.

Special Purpose Vehicles

One of the great things about bus design is that if needs be the bodies can be removed from the chassis and then replaced with whatever body the company or operator required. These conversions took on many unique and unusual forms, ranging from conversions designed to carry race cars internally and externally on the vehicle, through to being used as ambulances and emergency control/radio units, canteens and anything else that might have been required.

Built in 1940 as a double-decker for the Wallasey Corporation (No. 74), this Metropolitan-Cammell-bodied Leyland Titan TD7 was used as such until 1952 when it was sold to Wallasey Police, who converted it to a half-deck mobile incident control room; it was also used by the Cumberland Constabulary prior to preservation. It was seen at Winkleigh in Devon on 7 October 2012.

In 1948 London Transport Corporation had this OSS prime mover tractor unit (plus nine others) built for them by Scammell Ltd along with this trailer, one of thirteen and purpose built by Spurlings Coachbuilders Ltd to be used as a mobile staff canteen unit. It was withdrawn in 1959 and purchased by the Liverpool Corporation. The London Bus Museum acquired them both in 1973 on and the occasion of my visit on 20 October 2019 the restoration had been completed to original London Transport condition.

9

The Heart of the Matter

The majority of buses looked at in this book, along with those not covered by it, all have one thing in common: they are constructed as a lorry chassis fitted with various makers' or coachbuilders' bodies on them. Therefore, it is unmistakably the chassis that lies at the heart of these vehicles. It does, after all, contain the running gear, the engine and the axles, etc., without all of which the bodywork would be redundant and it would either just be a shed or nothing at all. This final chapter looks at some of those examples, without which this book would not exist.

Seen on display at the Oxford Bus Museum on 10 November 2019 was this 1915-built Daimler Y type chassis, which was originally used by the City of Oxford Electric Tramways Company as No. 39.

This petrol-electric chassis was built in 1922 by Tilling-Stevens as a type TS3A, and it was used by Southdown as No. 67. It is seen pictured on 11 July 2009, inside the workshop of the Amberley Museum.

Another Tilling-Stevens-built vehicle seen at Amberley on 9 July 2011 is this TS6 example, which was noted having its Short Brothers bodywork rebuilt onto it in the museum's workshop. It was new to the Maidstone & District Corporation as No. 73 in 1925.

VH 2088 was noted in a typical engineering workshop in West Yorkshire on 13 August 2016, surrounded by iron garden gates and radiators, etc. It was built in 1929 as a Karrier KA type. At the time of writing it is unknown to the author which company originally owned it.

Seen at the Trolleybus Museum at Sandtoft on 14 October 2017 is this Ransomes of Ipswich 1931-built D6 chassis. It was used by Nottingham Corporation with Brush bodywork as No. 46 until its withdrawal in 1950. It is a long-term restoration project at the museum and not a priority. Note the handbrake shaft.

City of Oxford Corporation No. GC41 is what this 1932-built AEC Regal 4 chassis once operated as. It is seen here on 10 November 2019 displayed at the Oxford Bus Museum. Note the missing rear wheels on the side nearest the camera.

New to the Manchester Corporation in 1934 as No. 526 was this Leyland Titan TD3. The chassis can be seen on display inside the Greater Manchester Museum of Transport, as was the case on 26 January 2013.

This Karrier E6A trolleybus chassis was built in 1938 and was new to the Huddersfield Corporation (No. 470) when it would have been fitted with Park Royal bodywork. It was withdrawn from service in 1953 and was noted awaiting restoration at Sandtoft on 14 October 2017. Note how the steering wheel and handbrake in situ give this vehicle a rather odd look.

Between 1939 and 1954, AEC built over 4,800 buses for London Transport. This example is a Regent III and dates from 1949 as No. RT 2213. It was withdrawn in 1969 and sold to the Cambridgeshire Burwell & District bus company and was converted to a mobile restaurant, then a children's shop. While awaiting restoration it was destroyed in an arson attack in 1994; the body remains were scrapped and the chassis was donated to the London Bus Museum, where they maintain it in a working condition (with all major parts labelled) for demonstration purposes. It was noted on 20 October 2019.

This rather rusty AEC Regal of an unidentified year was one of several vehicles that were sold at auction in 1990 in Taunton after having lain in a back garden for numerous years and left to nature. At the time of writing the history and current whereabouts of this vehicle are unknown to the author. It was pictured on the day of the auction, 17 February 1990.

Acknowledgements

The author would like to acknowledge the following museums/organisations for granting permission for images of their vehicles to be used within this publication:

National Brewery Centre, Museum of Brewing, Burton-on-Trent (www.nationalbrewerycentre.co.uk)

North East Land, Sea and Air Museum, Sunderland (www.melsam.org.uk)

National Motor Museum, Beaulieu (www.beaulieu.co.uk)

World of Country Life Museum, Sandy Bay (www.worldofcountrylife.co.uk)

Amberley Museum, Amberley (www.amberleymuseum.co.uk)

Milestones Museum, Basingstoke (www.milestonesmuseum.org.uk)

Wirral Transport Museum & Heritage Tramway, Birkenhead (www.wirraltransportmuseum.business.site)

The Living Museum of the North, Beamish (www.beamish.org.uk)

West of England Transport Collection, Winkleigh (www.wetc.uk.com)

Industrial Museum, Bradford (www.bradfordmuseums.org)

Other museums and places of interest included in this publication include:

Transport for London Museum and Depot Store, Covent Garden Piazza and Acton Town (www.ltmuseum.co.uk)

London Bus Museum, Weybridge (www.londonbusmuseum.com)

Black Country Living Museum, Dudley (www.bclm.co.uk)

Scottish Vintage Bus Museum, Dunfermline (www.svbm.online)

East Anglia Transport Museum, Carlton Colville (www.eatransportmuseum.co.uk)